# Rose Elliot's Book

C000225642

Rose Elliot is the author of s
cookbooks, and is renowned for her practical
and creative approach. She writes regularly
for the *Vegetarian* and has contributed to
national newspapers and magazines as well as
broadcasting on radio and television. She is
married and has three children.

Other titles available in the series

*Rose Elliot's Book of Beans and Lentils*
*Rose Elliot's Book of Breads*
*Rose Elliot's Book of Fruits*
*Rose Elliot's Book of Pasta*
*Rose Elliot's Book of Salads*
*Rose Elliot's Book of Savoury Flans and Pies*
*Rose Elliot's Book of Vegetables*

# Rose Elliot's Book of
# Cakes

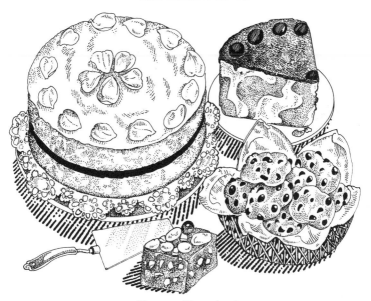

Fontana Paperbacks

First published by Fontana Paperbacks 1984

Set in 10 on 11pt Linotron Plantin
Drawings by Ken Lewis
except page 3 by Vana Haggerty
Made and printed in Great Britain by
William Collins Sons and Co. Ltd, Glasgow

# Introduction

Cakes are a pleasure to make: a welcome change from day-to-day cooking, a chance to produce a treat, to be indulgent for a special occasion. This book contains recipes for old favourites such as buttery Madeira cake, sticky gingerbread, featherlight sponge and rich Christmas cake, as well as some new ideas such as banana cake with curd cheese and raspberry filling and almond and cherry ring.

I know some people feel nervous about making cakes. But baking a cake is really just a chemical process and if you understand a few basic principles and follow a reliable recipe carefully, you really can't go wrong!

### EQUIPMENT

You need the usual weighing equipment, a large bowl, a wooden spoon, sieve and spatula for scraping the mixture from the sides of the bowl. An electric mixer or food processor speeds up the process but is not essential. You will need a thin skewer or cocktail stick for testing whether the cake is done and a wire rack for cooling the cake – use the biggest and strongest you can find.

It's worth buying good quality cake tins; I like the non-stick ones because these are heavy and strong, though they still need greasing, I find. A basic set of cake tins would be:

two 18–cm (7–in) sandwich tins with straight sides at least 2.5 cm (1 in) deep
one 20–cm (8–in) square tin with sides at least 4 cm (1½ in) deep, preferably with slightly rounded corners
one 18–cm (7–in), and one 20–cm (8–in) round tin with sides at least 7.5 cm (3 in) deep

With these you could make all the cakes in this book except for three. For the nutty fruit cake you need a 450–g (1–lb) loaf tin, for the swiss roll, a swiss roll tin, 33 x 23 cm (13 x 9 in) with sides at least 1.5 cm (1 in) deep, and a 20–cm (8–in) ring for the almond and cherry ring.

**Flour**
Soft flour, that is, flour milled from wheat containing less gluten, is best for cakes as it absorbs fat and produces a light, tender texture. Self-raising flour is most frequently used, but plain flour is needed for some cakes.

Wholewheat flour, or an 81 per cent wholewheat flour can be used

6

instead of white in any recipe; the finished cake will have the characteristic flavour and colour of wholewheat flour. Self-raising wholewheat flour can be bought at health shops. As long as you use self-raising or plain as specified in a recipe you can vary the 'brown-ness' of the flour according to your own preference.

## Raising agents

These are chemical mixtures which produce carbon dioxide when mixed with liquid. This expands when heated, forcing the cake to rise. Baking powder is the one most often used and is included in self-raising flour, though extra may be called for in the recipe. Bicarbonate of soda is also sometimes used.

## Other dry ingredients

Ground rice, cornflour, oatmeal, desiccated coconut, cocoa or carob may be added for flavour, replacing an equivalent amount of flour to keep the basic proportions.

## Fat

When beaten, fat traps air bubbles and these make the cake light; it also helps to tenderize the starch and gluten in the flour and keeps the cake moist during cooking. Butter gives the best flavour and is worth using for Christmas and wedding cakes, delicately flavoured Victoria sandwich cakes and Madeira cakes. Whipped margarine creams easily, gives light results and is generally used for quick all-in-one recipes (although soft butter can be used). White cooking fat or block margarine is best for cakes such as rock buns which are made by the rubbing-in method, and for strongly flavoured cakes like gingerbread. Oil can also be used; this, like lard, contains no water, so approximately one quarter less fat is needed, together with an extra raising agent to allow for the fact that there is no creaming process to aerate the mixture.

## Sugar
Like fat, this softens the gluten in the flour, making a tender cake. Used in the right proportions it helps the cake to rise and improves the flavour, appearance and keeping-qualities of the cake. Caster sugar or soft brown sugar are best for cake-making as they consist of very small granules which dissolve easily. From the health point of view there's no advantage in using real brown sugar; it's better simply to use less sugar (see the sugarless fruit cake recipe on page 60) or to make delicious traditional cakes but to keep them just for special treats.

## Liquid sweeteners
Honey, golden syrup and black treacle are sometimes used to replace a proportion of sugar in a recipe and are important ingredients in cakes such as gingerbread and parkin. They give a moist, dense texture.

**Eggs**
These improve the flavour, nutritional value and keeping-qualities of cakes. They also help to bind the ingredients together and to raise the mixture, trapping the air when they are beaten. Recipes are normally based on medium-sized or 'standard' eggs, size 3, about 50 g (2 oz) when weighed in the shell. They should be at room temperature (otherwise they may make the mixture curdle when added), so need to be removed from the fridge at least an hour in advance. It is, however, possible to make a surprisingly light cake without eggs: see recipe on page 56.

**Liquids**
Eggs, which are used in most cakes, contain a good deal of water, so for many recipes additional liquid is unnecessary. Sometimes a very little water or milk is added to give the right consistency. In cakes such as gingerbread, made by the melting method, milk may be added to give a batter-like consistency and some recipes, occasionally contain soured milk which helps the cake to rise. Orange and lemon juice, strained tea, brandy, rum and sherry are other liquids which are sometimes used.

**Dried fruit**
Currants, raisins, sultanas, candied peel and dates can all be used; also prunes and dried apricots, pears and peaches. Most dried fruit is ready-washed, but glacé fruits such as cherries and pineapple,

angelica and crystallized ginger, need washing to remove excess sugar. Pat these dry, halve glacé cherries (as their weight can cause them to sink in the mixture), and chop the others.

## Nuts
Chopped and ground nuts make a delicious addition to cakes; almonds, hazel nuts, cashews, walnuts and brazils are all useful.

## Additional flavourings
Essences, such as vanilla and almond can be added; these are concentrated, so need measuring carefully. Coffee essence may be used, or a good quality instant coffee dissolved in a little water. Grated orange and lemon rind are also good, but be careful about using the juice (unless specified in the recipe) as the acidity can affect the raising agents and the cake may not rise properly.

MAKING THE CAKE

## 1 Preparing the cake tins
For perfect results, it's important to use tins of the size specified in the recipe; while you can improvise, this may affect the timing of the cake and the way in which it cooks. The cake tin needs to be greased lightly but thoroughly with melted butter or flavourless cooking oil, lined with greaseproof paper and re-greased. The drawings on pages 11 and 12 show how to line the different shapes of tin.

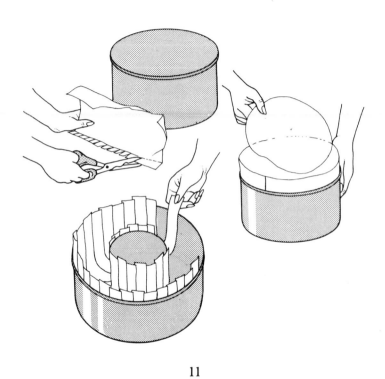

11

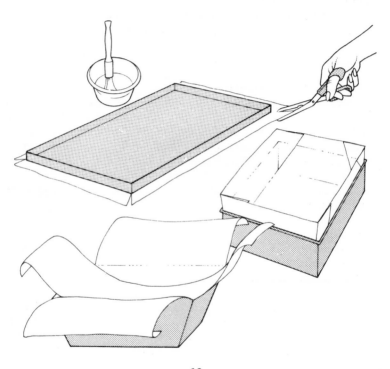

## 2 Preparing the oven

Always position the oven shelf in the centre, unless you have a fan-assisted oven or the recipe specifies otherwise. Set the oven to the temperature given. It is important that the oven should have reached the correct heat when the cake is put in.

## 3 Preparing the ingredients

Prepare the ingredients as indicated in the recipe: sift the flour with the baking powder, if used, and other dry ingredients such as cocoa and spices. This aerates the flour and ensures there are no lumps. If you are using wholewheat flour, sift as much through the sieve as you can, then add the residue of bran from the sieve. Make sure eggs are at room temperature and beat them if required; chop fruit and nuts as necessary; wash crystallized fruit; melt chocolate; dissolve coffee powder in water.

## 4 Mixing the cake

Cake-making is based on several simple methods, the names of which refer to the way in which ingredients are incorporated: creaming, all-in-one, rubbing in, melting, and whisking.

*Creaming* Here the fat is beaten with the sugar until pale and fluffy. This releases the flavour from the butter and incorporates air, resulting in a light cake. Next, any liquid flavourings or citrus zest are added, then the eggs, which must be beaten in gradually to prevent

the mixture from curdling. If it does curdle, add a little flour and continue. The cake will still taste good, but the texture won't be quite so good. When all the egg has been beaten in, the sifted flour is added using a technique called folding. To do this, add a third of the flour to the creamed mixture and with a metal spoon carefully cut and turn the creamed mixture over the flour until it is incorporated, then repeat until it has all been added (see drawing on page 15). Then lightly mix in any other ingredients. The mixture should have a soft-dropping consistency. This means that it drops easily off the spoon when lifted just above the bowl. It may be necessary to add a little liquid in order to achieve this: water gives the lightest results.

*All-in-one* As the name implies, all the ingredients are placed in a bowl and mixed together until they're light and slightly glossy. The short amount of beating means a limited amount of air is incorporated so extra baking powder is added to compensate.

*Rubbing-in* Here the flour and any raising agents and spices are sifted into a large bowl, then the fat is rubbed into the flour until the mixture resembles fine breadcrumbs. Then the other ingredients are added and mixed gently until blended. The mixture may be stiffer than the soft-dropping consistency of sponge cake mixtures, particularly for small cakes such as rock buns which are baked on a baking sheet and so need to be able to hold their shape. For these the mixture needs to just hold together and will cling to the spoon.

15

*Melting* This is a simple method used for cakes with a sticky texture such as gingerbread. The fat, sugar and other sweeteners such as treacle, honey or golden syrup are melted over a gentle heat. When the pan is cool enough to touch, the melted mixture is added to the dry ingredients, together with any additional liquid or egg and mixed well. The consistency should be batter-like.

*Whisking* This is used to make sponges which contain no fat or only a small amount. The eggs and sugar are put into a large bowl set over a saucepan of very hot water and whisked until pale and thick. This takes about 10 minutes with an electric hand whisk and about 15 minutes by hand. Alternatively, the eggs and sugar can be whisked with a table mixer without standing the bowl over hot water. The mixture is ready as soon as the whisk, when lifted out of the mixture, will leave a trail which remains for at least 3 seconds. Then the flour is folded in gently, a quarter at a time, and finally any melted butter or liquid stated in the recipe.

**5 Putting the mixture into the tin(s)**
Once the mixture has been made it should be baked as soon as possible. Spoon the mixture into the tin(s), using a spatula to scrape down the sides of the bowl. Level the surface with the back of a spoon. In the case of rich fruit cakes, make a slight hollow in the centre to compensate for the rising and give the cake a flat top.

## 6 Baking the cake

Put the cake into the pre-heated oven. Once the cake is in the oven, don't open the oven door until the end of the minimum baking time given in the recipe. This is most important; if you do, cold air will enter the oven and the cake will probably sink in the middle. This is one of the most common reasons for unsuccessful cakes.

## 7 Testing whether the cake is done

The cake should be well risen, evenly browned and the sides should have shrunk away from the tin. Light sponge cakes should spring back when lightly touched with a fingertip; if any impression is left, the cake needs more baking. Fruit cakes and other deep cakes should be tested by inserting a thin skewer or cocktail stick in the centre. It should come out clean. If there is any uncooked mixture clinging to it, the cake needs to cook longer.

## 8 Cooling the cake

When you take the cake out of the oven, let it stand in its tin for a short while: 30 seconds for a sponge sandwich cake, 2–5 minutes for other cakes, then turn the cake out on to a wire rack with a tea cloth on top. Remove cake tin and paper, then pick up the cake and the tea towel and put the cake back on the rack the right way up. Leave until completely cold.

## 9 Storing and freezing

Cakes should be kept in an airtight container: a tin is best. Whisked sponges and plain cakes made by the rubbing-in method are best eaten the day they are made, but will keep for 2–3 days. All-in-one creamed sponges will keep for about 3 days; sponges made by the traditional method, for 6–7 days. Gingerbread and Dundee cake keep for up to 3 weeks (or more) whilst Christmas cake will keep for several weeks at least, if sprinkled with brandy, wrapped in two layers of greaseproof paper and stored in an airtight tin.

Cakes which may be frozen are shown by the symbol Ⓕ. Sandwich cakes and sponges freeze well, either plain or decorated. Wrap undecorated cakes in polythene or foil; open-freeze decorated cakes then pack carefully in plastic containers. Freeze for up to 2 months. To use, remove wrappings while cakes are still frozen, then stand cakes on a wire rack to thaw.

FILLING AND ICING THE CAKE

While some cakes such as gingerbread, Dundee cake and Madeira cake are perfect served as they are, others can be enhanced with a complementary filling and icing. And if you're artistically inclined you can have fun decorating the cake. You will need a short palette knife, or knife with a wide, straight blade. A nylon piping bag fitted with a medium-sized shell nozzle is useful for adding an attractive finishing touch, but not essential.

**Fillings**
Jam is perhaps the easiest and most traditional filling for a sponge; try experimenting with different flavours. The reduced sugar jams which you can buy at health shops and some supermarkets are excellent, also lemon curd and thick fruit purées. Whipped cream or buttercream are both delicious, as is curd cheese: see recipe on page 24.

**Toppings**
The simplest topping is a sprinkling of caster sugar or icing sugar. If you put a paper doily on top of the cake before sifting the icing sugar over, you will get a pretty pattern. Or the cake can be coated with melted chocolate or carob bar, with glacé or fudge icing, buttercream, curd cheese icing or seven-minute frosting: see pages 23–26.

They can then be decorated with colourful items such as crystallized violet and rose petals, pistachio nuts, angelica, walnuts, almonds, hazel nuts, crystallized orange and lemon sections, grated and flaked chocolate.

**To coat a cake with almond paste** (see drawing on page 20)
Make sure the cake is level: trim with a sharp knife if necessary. Sieve about 3 tablespoons apricot jam and melt gently in a small saucepan. Use a piece of string to measure all round the outside of the cake, and another to measure its depth. Roll two thirds of the almond paste into a rectangle half the length of the cake and twice

the depth, then cut in half lengthwise. Brush each piece with melted apricot jam. Roll the cake on to the strips to cover the sides and press together the joins. Roll out remaining almond paste to fit the top. Brush with jam, place on top of cake and roll gently with a rolling pin. Roll a straight-sided jam jar around the outside of the cake to help the almond paste to stick. Leave in a cool airy place to dry before applying the icing: ideally 2–3 days if you're going to eat the cake quickly, 6–7 days for one you're going to keep longer.

**To rough-ice a fruit cake**
Put all the icing on top of the cake and roll it backwards and forwards with a palette knife a few times to remove air bubbles. Then spread evenly over the cake. Finally use the blade of the knife to rough up the icing into peaks (see drawing, page 22). The cake can be decorated with silver balls, bought decorations or shapes cut or moulded from coloured almond paste. A winter birthday cake looks pretty with a candle in the middle surrounded by almond paste leaves and fruits: see drawing on page 22.

# Almond Paste

MAKES SUFFICIENT TO COVER A 20–23 CM (8–9 IN) CAKE

450 g (1 lb) ground almonds
225 g (8 oz) caster sugar
225 g (8 oz) icing sugar

1 teaspoon lemon juice
few drops almond essence
2 eggs, beaten

Put the ground almonds and caster sugar into a bowl, then sift in the icing sugar and mix together. Add lemon juice, essence and enough egg (you may not need it all) to make a smooth, firm paste. Knead lightly; use immediately.

# Simple Buttercream

SUFFICIENT TO TOP AND FILL, OR COAT, AN 18–CM (7–IN) CAKE

125 g (4 oz) icing sugar or soft
  brown sugar

50 g (2 oz) softened butter
1–2 tablespoons hot water

Sift icing sugar. Beat butter until light, then add icing sugar or soft brown sugar and beat again, adding enough liquid to make a light consistency.

For chocolate buttercream, add 50 g (2 oz) melted chocolate or 1 tablespoon cocoa dissolved in the hot water. For coffee buttercream, 2 teaspoons instant coffee dissolved in the hot water. For orange or lemon buttercream, add the grated rind and mix with orange or lemon juice instead of water. For vanilla buttercream, add a few drops of vanilla essence, and for a reduced sugar buttercream replace 50 g (2 oz) of the icing sugar with 50 g (2 oz) dried skim milk powder or granules; beat well until smooth.

# Curd Cheese Icing

ENOUGH TO FILL AND TOP AN 18–CM (7–IN) CAKE

125 g (4 oz) curd cheese
25 g (1 oz) icing sugar
few drops vanilla essence

25 g (1 oz) unsalted butter or
 margarine

Beat together until smooth and creamy.

# Fudge Icing

TO TOP AND FILL, OR COAT, AN 18–CM (7–IN) CAKE

40 g (1½ oz) butter
2 tablespoons water

175 g (6 oz) icing sugar
few drops vanilla essence

*Lemon Juice for lemon icing*

Heat butter and water gently until melted. Remove from heat and sift in the icing sugar. Add vanilla essence, beat well. The icing will thicken up as it cools.

Flavour can be varied as for simple buttercream.

# Glacé Icing

ENOUGH TO COAT THE TOP OF AN 18–CM (7–IN) CAKE

125 g (4 oz) sifted icing sugar

1–2 tablespoons warm water

Sift icing sugar into a bowl, then add water and beat until smooth and glossy. Use at once.

25

# Royal Icing

| | |
|---|---|
| 900 g (2 lb) icing sugar | 1 tablespoon lemon juice |
| 4 egg whites | 2 teaspoons glycerine |

Sift icing sugar. Put egg whites into a bowl and whisk until just frothy. Then add the icing sugar a little at a time, beating well after each addition. When about half has been added, beat in the lemon juice. When all the icing sugar has been added beat in the glycerine.

# Seven-minute Frosting

SUFFICIENT TO COAT AN 18–CM (7–IN) ROUND CAKE; USE DOUBLE FOR A 23–CM (9–IN) ROUND CAKE.

| | |
|---|---|
| 1 large egg white | pinch of salt |
| 6 oz caster sugar | pinch of cream of tartar |
| 2 tablespoons water | |

Put all the ingredients into a bowl and whisk until foamy. Set bowl over a pan of simmering water (but make sure bowl does not touch water) and whisk until mixture stands in soft peaks: about 7 minutes. Use icing at once, leave to set.

Recipes marked (F) show cakes which are suitable for freezing

# All-in-one Fruit Cake

MAKES ONE 20–CM (8–IN) CAKE Ⓕ

225 g (8 oz) self-raising flour
175 g (6 oz) soft margarine
175 g (6 oz) soft brown sugar
3 eggs

350 g (12 oz) mixed dried fruit
125 g (4 oz) glacé cherries,
    halved

Set oven to 160°C (325°F), gas mark 3. Grease and line a 20–cm (8–in) deep round cake tin. Sift flour into a large mixing bowl; add the rest of the ingredients. Beat with a wooden spoon or electric mixer for 2–3 minutes, until everything is well combined and mixture is thick and creamy. Turn into prepared tin, smooth top. Bake for 2–2½ hours. Cool in tin for 3 minutes, then turn cake out on to a wire rack, gently peel off paper and leave to cool.

For special occasions, make a glazed jewelled topping: brush top of cake with warmed honey, cover with circles of halved glacé cherries, nuts and dates, brush with more honey. Topping can also be used on Christmas cakes.

# All-in-one Sponge

125 g (4 oz) self-raising flour
1 teaspoon baking powder
125 g (4 oz) soft margarine or
    butter

125 g (4 oz) caster sugar or soft
    brown sugar
2 eggs
1–2 tablespoons water

*For the filling*
3 tablespoons jam
caster sugar or icing sugar to
    dredge

Set oven to 160°C (325°F), gas mark 3. Grease and base-line two 18–cm (7–in) sandwich tins. Sift flour and baking powder into a large mixing bowl, add margarine or butter, sugar and eggs. Beat for 2–3 minutes, until mixture is light and glossy. Add water a little at a time, if necessary, to make a soft, dropping consistency. Divide mixture between the two tins, smooth tops. Bake for 35 minutes, until centre of cake springs back when touched lightly. Cool for 30 seconds, then turn cakes on to a wire rack, strip off paper and leave to cool. Sandwich cakes with jam and sift a little icing sugar on top or sprinkle with caster sugar.

# Almond and Cherry Ring

MAKES ONE 20–CM (8–IN) CAKE (F)

A pretty cake baked in the shape of a ring and flavoured with almonds and cherries.

150 g (5 oz) self-raising flour
50 g (2 oz) glacé cherries
175 g (6 oz) butter
175 g (6 oz) caster sugar
3 eggs, beaten

50 g (2 oz) ground almonds
few drops almond essence
1 quantity glacé icing (page 25)
25 g (1 oz) toasted flaked
  almonds

Set oven to 180°C (350°F), gas mark 4. Line and grease a 20–cm (8–in) ring tin (see page 11). Sift flour. Rinse cherries, slice half and keep on one side. Chop remainder. Cream butter and sugar until light, gradually beat in the egg. Fold in flour, ground almonds, chopped cherries and essence. Spoon into tin, smooth top, bake for 55–60 minutes. Remove from tin, strip off paper, cool. Spoon icing over top of cake, decorate with the reserved sliced cherries and toasted almonds.

# Banana Cake with Curd Cheese and Raspberry Filling

A moist, light banana-flavoured cake with an unusual filling.

MAKES ONE 18–CM (7–IN) CAKE

125 g (4 oz) self-raising flour
1 teaspoon baking powder
125 g (4 oz) soft margarine or
  butter

125 g (4 oz) soft brown sugar
2 eggs
1 medium-sized banana, peeled
  and mashed

*For filling and topping*
125 g (4 oz) curd cheese
2 tablespoons double cream
1 teaspoon soft brown sugar

1 heaped tablespoon raspberry
  jam
caster sugar to dredge

Bake the cake as described on page 30, mixing the mashed banana with the other ingredients. While the cake is cooking make the curd cheese filling: beat together the curd cheese, cream and sugar until light and thick. Spread one of the cakes with the jam then with the curd cheese mixture; place second cake on top, dredge with caster sugar. Eat the same day.

# Bramble Cream Cake

Pretty for a special tea, this cake is filled and topped with shiny red bramble jelly and finished with a lattice of whipped cream.

MAKES ONE 18–CM (7–IN) SANDWICH CAKE

| | |
|---|---|
| 125 g (4 oz) self-raising flour | 2 eggs |
| 1 teaspoon baking powder | 1–2 tablespoons water |
| 125 g (4 oz) soft butter or margarine | 3 tablespoons bramble jelly |
| | 150 ml (¼ pint) double cream |
| 125 g (4 oz) caster sugar or soft brown sugar | 1 tablespoon milk |

Set oven to 160°C (325°F), gas mark 3. Grease and line two 18–cm (7–in) sandwich tins. Make cake exactly as described for all-in-one sponge on page 30; bake and cool. Gently melt bramble jelly. Whip cream with the milk until it stands in peaks. Sandwich cakes with 1 tablespoon of the jam and half the cream. Pour and spread remaining jelly over top of cake. Put rest of cream into a piping bag fitted with a medium-sized shell nozzle. Pipe a border of shells round edge of cake, then a trellis pattern over top.

# Butterfly Cakes

MAKES 15 (F)

125 g (4 oz) self-raising flour
1 teaspoon baking powder
125 g (4 oz) soft margarine or
  butter

125 g (4 oz) caster sugar or soft
  brown sugar
2 medium-sized eggs
1–2 tablespoons water

*For the decoration*
1 quantity buttercream (page
  23), or curd cheese filling
  (page 24)

icing sugar to dredge
15 paper cake cases

Set oven to 190°C (375°F), gas mark 5. Make an all-in-one sponge mix as described on page 30 and put a heaped teaspoonful in each cake case. Bake just below centre of oven for 20–25 minutes, until golden brown. Cool on wire rack. When cakes are cold, cut a thin slice, horizontally, from the top of each, then cut slice in half and leave on one side. Spoon or pipe a dollop of buttercream on top of each cake, then press the two cut pieces on top like butterfly wings. Pipe or spoon any remaining buttercream decoratively between the 'wings'. Dredge with icing sugar.

# Carrot Cake

Curd cheese icing or buttercream make good alternatives to the topping given.

MAKES ONE 20–CM (8–IN) SQUARE CUTTING INTO 12–16 PIECES

2 eggs, separated
100 g (3½ oz) soft brown sugar
100 g (3½ oz) finely chopped or
    grated carrot

100 g (3½ oz) finely chopped or
    grated hazel nuts

*For topping*
75 g (3 oz) chocolate or carob
    bar, broken up

15 g (½ oz) butter
1 tablespoon water

Grease and line a 20–cm (8–in) square tin. Set oven to 180°C (350°F), gas mark 4. Put egg yolks into a bowl with the sugar and whisk until thick and light. Fold in the grated carrot and hazel nut. Whisk the egg whites until stiff then fold into the mixture. Pour into prepared tin, gently level top. Bake for 30–35 minutes, until centre springs back when touched lightly. Cool on a wire rack. Melt chocolate or carob in a small bowl over a pan of hot water, beat in butter and water, then spread over the top of the cake; cut into slices when set.

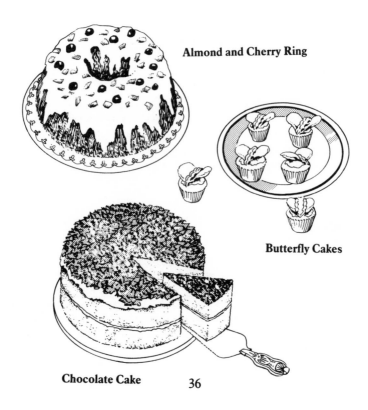

**Almond and Cherry Ring**

**Butterfly Cakes**

**Chocolate Cake**

36

# Chocolate Cake

Luscious chocolate cake is irresistible and this one is easy to make.

MAKES ONE 18–CM (7–IN) CAKE (F)

125 g (4 oz) self-raising flour
1 tablespoon cocoa
1 teaspoon baking powder
1 – 2 tablespoons water
125 g (4 oz) soft margarine or
   butter

125 g (4 oz) caster sugar or soft
   brown sugar
2 eggs
1–2 tablespoons warm water

*For filling, icing and decoration*
1 quantity chocolate
buttercream or fudge icing, page
   23–24

25 g (1 oz) coarsely grated
   chocolate
icing sugar to dredge

Make the cake according to the recipe on page 30, sifting the cocoa with the flour and adding enough water to make a soft-dropping consistency. Bake and cool as described. When the cake is cool, sandwich with half chocolate buttercream or fudge icing. Spread remainder over top, then press grated chocolate on top and dredge with icing sugar.

# Christmas Cake

MAKES ONE 20–CM (8–IN) CAKE Ⓕ

175 g (6 oz) plain flour
1 teaspoon mixed spice
175 g (6 oz) soft butter
175 g (6 oz) soft brown sugar
5 eggs, beaten
1 tablespoon treacle
grated rind and juice of
    1 lemon
700 g (1½ lb) mixed dried fruit

75 g (3 oz) chopped glacé
    pineapple
125 g (4 oz) glacé cherries,
    halved
75 g (3 oz) ground almonds
40 g (1½ oz) chopped blanched
    almonds
1 tablespoon brandy

Set oven to 140°C (275°F), gas mark 1. Grease a 20–cm (8–in) round cake tin; line with greased greaseproof paper. Sift flour and spice. Cream butter and sugar; gradually beat in eggs. Stir in treacle, then fold in flour. Gently mix in lemon juice and rind, dried and glacé fruit and nuts. Turn into tin, hollow centre slightly. Bake for 4½–5 hours. Cool on wire rack. Prick top of cake and sprinkle with brandy. Wrap in greaseproof paper, store in tin until ready for icing.

# Coconut and Orange Cake

MAKES ONE 20–CM (8–IN) ROUND CAKE Ⓕ

225 g (8 oz) self-raising flour
2 teaspoons baking powder
50 g (2 oz) desiccated coconut
225 g (8 oz) soft margarine or
   butter

225 g (8 oz) soft brown sugar
4 eggs
grated rind of 1 orange

*To finish and decorate*
1 quantity of orange glacé icing
   (page 25)

a little grated orange rind and
   toasted coconut strands

Set oven to 180°C (350°F), gas mark 4. Line and grease a 20–cm (8–in) deep cake tin. Sift flour and baking powder into a large bowl. Add coconut, margarine or butter, soft brown sugar, eggs and orange rind and mix well for 2–3 minutes, until thick, smooth and slightly glossy. Turn into tin, smooth top and bake for about 1 hour, until a skewer inserted into the centre comes out clean. Cool on wire rack. When cake is cold, spoon icing over the top and sprinkle with grated orange rind and a few strands of toasted coconut.

39

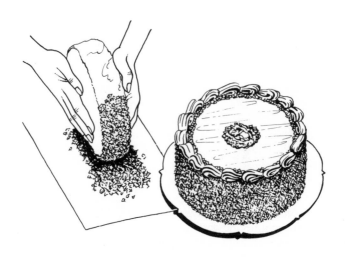

# Coffee and Walnut Cake

MAKES ONE 18–CM (7–IN) CAKE Ⓕ

125 g (4 oz) self-raising flour
1 teaspoon baking powder
125 g (4 oz) soft margarine or
    butter
125 g (4 oz) caster sugar or soft
    brown sugar

1 tablespoon instant coffee
    dissolved in 1 tablespoon
    water
2 eggs

*For the filling and topping*
double quantity coffee-flavoured
    buttercream, page 23
50 g (2 oz) walnuts, finely
chopped

walnut pieces

Make cake exactly as described on page 30, adding the coffee mixture with the eggs. Bake and cool. Put two tablespoons buttercream into a piping bag fitted with a medium-sized nozzle. Sandwich cake with a third of remaining buttercream. Spread sides of cake with half rest of buttercream then coat in chopped walnuts: see drawing on page 40. Cover top of cake with remaining buttercream, decorate with swirls of piping and walnuts as shown on page 40.

# Dundee Cake

This traditional cake has a delicious crumbly texture. I like to use wholewheat flour, but you could substitute white if you prefer.

MAKES ONE 20–CM (8–IN) ROUND CAKE Ⓕ

225 g (8 oz) plain wholewheat flour
1 teaspoon baking powder
175 g (6 oz) soft butter
175 g (6 oz) soft brown sugar
grated rind of 1 lemon

3 eggs, beaten
300 g (10 oz) mixed dried fruit
50 g (2 oz) glacé cherries, halved
25 g (1 oz) ground almonds
50 g (2 oz) blanched almonds for topping

Set oven to 160°C (325°F), gas mark 3. Grease and line a 20–cm (8–in) deep round tin. Sift flour and baking powder. Cream butter and sugar until light, add lemon rind. Gradually beat in eggs. Fold in sifted flour, then dried fruit, cherries and ground almonds. Spoon into tin, hollow centre slightly. Arrange blanched almonds lightly on top. Bake for 2– 2½ hours, until a skewer inserted in centre comes out clean. Cool on wire rack.

# Frosted Walnut Layer Cake

MAKES ONE 20–CM (8–IN) ROUND CAKE

225 g (8 oz) self-raising flour
175 g (6 oz) softened butter
175 g (6 oz) soft brown sugar
2 teaspoons strong instant coffee
   dissolved in 1 tablespoon
   water

3 eggs, beaten
50 g (2 oz) chopped walnuts
double quantity frosting, page
   26
9 walnut halves to decorate

Set oven to 160°C (325°F), gas mark 3. Grease and fully line a deep 20–cm (8–in) cake tin. Sift flour. Cream butter and sugar until light and fluffy. Add coffee, then gradually add egg, beating well. Fold in flour and walnut. Add water if necessary to make soft, dropping consistency. Turn mixture into tin, smooth top and bake for 1–1¼ hours. Cool on wire rack. Cut cake horizontally into three equal layers. Spread a quarter of the frosting over the bottom layer, place second layer on top, repeat with remaining layer. Coat sides and top with rest of frosting; decorate with one walnut half in the centre and the rest round the edge.

# Gingerbread

This moist, sticky gingerbread can be varied by the addition of 50 g (2 oz) chopped crystallized ginger, or by sprinkling some nuts on top before baking.

MAKES A 20 –CM (8–IN) SQUARE CUTTING INTO 12 PIECES (F)

225 g (8 oz) plain wholewheat
  flour
2 teaspoons ground ginger
1 teaspoon bicarbonate of soda
125 g (4 oz) golden syrup

125 g (4 oz) black treacle
75 g (3 oz) white cooking fat
125 g (4 oz) soft brown sugar
1 egg, beaten
150 ml (5 fl oz) milk

Set oven to 160°C (325°F), gas mark 3. Grease and line a 20–cm (8–in) square tin. Sift flour, ginger and bicarbonate of soda into a large bowl. Put syrup, treacle, fat and sugar into a saucepan and heat gently until melted. Cool until you can comfortably place your hand against the pan, then add the egg and milk and mix well. Add to dry ingredients; stir thoroughly. Pour into tin, bake for 1¼ hours until well risen and firm to the touch. Cool on wire rack.

**Frosted Walnut Layer Cake**

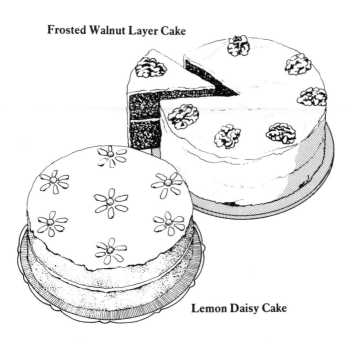

**Lemon Daisy Cake**

# Lemon Daisy Cake

A pretty fresh-tasting cake with a pattern of daisies on top.

MAKES ONE 18–CM (7–IN) CAKE Ⓕ

125 g (4 oz) self-raising flour
1 teaspoon baking powder
125 g (4 oz) soft margarine
125 g (4 oz) caster sugar or soft
   brown sugar

grated rind of 1 lemon
2 eggs, beaten
1–2 tablespoons water

*For icing and decoration*
lemon fudge icing, page 25
mimosa balls

a few blanched almonds

Make the cake as described for the all-in-one sponge on page 30, adding the lemon rind before the eggs. Bake and cool. Spread one sponge with half the icing, place other half on top and spread with remaining icing. Arrange the mimosa balls and blanched almonds on top to resemble daisies: see drawing on page 45.

# Madeira Cake

This traditional golden cake has a deliciously tender texture and buttery flavour.

MAKES ONE 18–CM (7–IN) ROUND CAKE (F)

125 g (4 oz) plain flour
125 g (4 oz) self-raising flour
175 g (6 oz) softened butter

175 g (6oz) caster sugar
4 eggs
2 thin slices of citron peel

Set oven to 180°C (350°F), gas mark 4. Grease and line an 18–cm (7–in) deep round cake tin. Sift flours together. Cream the butter and sugar until very light and fluffy, then gradually add the eggs, beating well after each addition. Fold in the sifted flour. Spoon mixture into tin, smooth top. Bake for 30 minutes, then carefully open oven and place peel on top of cake, without removing cake from oven. Bake for a further 1–1¼ hours, until a skewer inserted into the centre comes out clean. Turn out on a wire rack to cool.

# Marble Cake

Chocolate and vanilla mixtures give this cake a marbled appearance when sliced: attractive for a child's birthday cake.

MAKES ONE 18–CM (7–IN) ROUND CAKE (F)

175 g (6 oz) self-raising flour
175 g (6 oz) soft margarine or
    butter
175 g (6 oz) caster sugar
3 eggs, beaten
½ teaspoon vanilla essence

1 tablespoon cocoa
1 tablespoon water
1 quantity chocolate fudge icing,
    page 25 – optional
chocolate flake or buttons –
    optional

Set oven to 180°C (350°F), gas mark 4. Grease and line a deep 18–cm (7–in) round cake tin. Sift flour. Cream margarine or butter and sugar until fluffy, then gradually add egg, beating well. Fold in flour and vanilla. Remove half mixture to another bowl, then fold cocoa and water into remaining mixture. Put alternate spoonfuls of chocolate and vanilla mixtures into the cake tin. Gently smooth top. Bake for 1–1¼ hours. Cool on wire rack. If liked, ice when cold and decorate with chocolate flake or buttons.

# Mocha Cake

This luscious cake works well with 81 per cent wholewheat flour.

MAKES ONE 18–CM (7–IN) SANDWICH CAKE Ⓕ

125 g (4 oz) self-raising flour
1 tablespoon cocoa
1 teaspoon baking powder
125 g (4 oz) soft butter or
 margarine

125 g (4 oz) soft brown sugar
2 eggs
2 teaspoons instant coffee
1 tablespoon water

*For icing*
1½ quantity chocolate
 buttercream, page 23

1 tablespoon instant coffee
sugar coffee beans to decorate

Set oven to 170°C (325°F), gas mark 3. Grease and line two 18–cm (7–in) sandwich tins. Make cake exactly as described for all-in-one sponge on page 30, sifting cocoa with flour and adding coffee dissolved in the water; bake and cool. Make the chocolate buttercream as described on page 23, using 175 g (6 oz) icing sugar, and adding the coffee, dissolved in the hot water. Sandwich cakes with a third of the mixture, spread rest over top and sides. Decorate with sugar coffee beans.

# Nutty Fruit Cake

A friend of mine makes this unusual cake as an alternative Christmas cake.

MAKES ONE 450–G (1–LB) LOAF CAKE Ⓕ

| | |
|---|---|
| 225 g (8 oz) dates | 40 g (1½ oz) plain flour |
| 225 g (8 oz) brazil nuts | ¼ teaspoon baking powder |
| 125 g (4 oz) glacé cherries | 1 large egg, beaten |
| 50 g (2 oz) soft brown sugar | ½ teaspoon vanilla essence |

Grease and line a 450–g (1–lb) loaf tin. Set oven to 150°C (300°F), gas mark 2. Chop dates, brazil nuts and glacé cherries, keeping whole a few of each for decoration. Put chopped nuts and fruit into a large bowl with the sugar. Sift in the flour and baking powder. Add egg and vanilla. Mix together. Spoon mixture into loaf tin, putting reserved dates, nuts and cherries on top. Press down lightly. Bake for 1¼–1½ hours, covering the top with greaseproof paper towards the end if it's getting too brown. Turn out carefully, cool on wire rack.

# Parkin

A simple recipe for a sticky, well-flavoured parkin. It gets stickier if wrapped in foil and stored for 2–7 days.

MAKES ONE 20–CM (8–IN) SQUARE CUTTING INTO 12 PIECES (F)

| | |
|---|---|
| 125 g (4 oz) plain wholewheat flour | 75 g (3 oz) soft brown sugar |
| 2 teaspoons baking powder | 125 g (4 oz) black treacle |
| 2 teaspoons ground ginger | 125 g (4 oz) golden syrup |
| 125 g (4 oz) medium oatmeal | 125 g (4 oz) margarine |
| | 175 ml (6 fl oz) milk |

Set oven to 180°C (350°F), gas mark 4. Grease and line a 20–cm (8–in) square tin. Sift flour, baking powder and ginger into a bowl and add the oatmeal. Put the sugar, treacle, syrup and margarine into a pan and heat gently until melted. Cool until you can comfortably place your hand against the pan, then stir in the milk. Add this mixture to the dry ingredients and mix well. Pour into tin, bake for 50–60 minutes, until firm to the touch. Cool on a wire rack. Cut into squares when cold.

# Rock Cakes

These spicy buns are quick to make and delicious eaten warm from the oven.

MAKES 8 CAKES (F)

225 g (8 oz) plain wholewheat flour
2 teaspoons baking powder
1 teaspoon mixed spice
50 g (2 oz) butter, cut in pieces
50 g (2 oz) white cooking fat, cut in pieces
75 g (3 oz) soft brown sugar
125 g (4 oz) mixed dried fruit
1 egg, beaten
1–2 tablespoons milk

Set oven to 220°C (425°F), gas mark 7. Grease a baking sheet. Sift the flour, baking powder and spice into a large bowl. Add the fats and rub in with your fingertips until the mixture looks like fine breadcrumbs, then use a fork to stir in the sugar, dried fruit and egg. The mixture should be fairly stiff and just hold together: add milk only if necessary to achieve this. Place tablespoons of the mixture about 4 cm (1½ in) apart on baking tray. Bake for 15 minutes, until golden brown and firm. Cool on tray for 5 minutes then transfer to wire rack.

# Rose Cake

This pretty pink cake with a rose-flavoured icing is lovely for a summer birthday.

MAKES ONE 18–CM (7–IN) SANDWICH CAKE

125 g (4 oz) self-raising flour
1 teaspoon baking powder
125 g (4 oz) soft butter or
    margarine
125 g (4 oz) caster sugar
2 eggs
1–2 tablespoons water
2 tablespoons raspberry jam
    and/or 2 heaped tablespoons
    whipped cream

1 quantity of glacé icing,
    coloured pale pink and made
    with rose water instead of
    water, or flavoured with rose
    essence
crystallized rose petals

Set oven to 160°C (325°F), gas mark 3. Grease and line two 18–cm (7–in) sandwich tins. Make cake exactly as described for all-in-one sponge on page 30; bake and cool. Sandwich cakes with the jam and/or the cream, then spread the pink icing over the top and decorate with the crystallized rose petals.

# Simnel Cake

A traditional favourite for Mothering Sunday and Easter.

MAKES ONE 20–CM (8–IN) CAKE

225 g (8 oz) plain wholewheat
    flour
1 teaspoon baking powder
175 g (6 oz) soft butter
175 g (6 oz) soft brown sugar
3 eggs, beaten
300 g (10 oz) mixed dried fruit

50 g (2 oz) glacé cherries, halved
1 quantity almond paste, page 23
2 tablespoons warmed sieved
    apricot jam
1 quantity white glacé icing,
    page 25
ribbon, small Easter eggs and
    chicks

Set oven to 160°C (325°F), gas mark 3, prepare tin and make cake mixture as described on page 42. Put half mixture in tin. Roll one third of almond paste into a circle 20 cm (8 in) across. Place on top of cake mixture, cover with remaining mixture. Smooth top, bake for 2–2½ hours. Cool, then brush with apricot jam. Roll half remaining almond paste into circle to fit top, press in place. Roll rest into 13 balls, place round edge of cake then brown under grill. Pour icing into centre, decorate as in drawing on page 54.

# Sponge Cake Without Eggs

The first time I made this I was amazed what an excellent cake it was possible to make without eggs. I make this cake a good deal because I have a daughter who doesn't eat eggs.

MAKES ONE 18–CM (7–IN) CAKE Ⓕ

225 g (8 oz) self-raising 81 per cent wholewheat flour
2 teaspoons baking powder
175 g (6 oz) caster sugar or soft brown sugar
6 tablespoons oil
225 ml (8 fl oz) water

1 teaspoon vanilla essence
2 heaped tablespoons jam and caster sugar to dredge, or 1 quantity fudge icing, page 25, or buttercream, page 23

Set oven to 180°C (350°F), gas mark 4. Grease and base-line two 18–cm (7–in) sandwich tins. Sift flour and baking powder into a bowl. Add caster sugar, then stir in oil, water and vanilla essence. Mix to a smooth batter-like consistency; pour into the tins. Bake for 25–30 minutes, until centre springs back to a light touch. Turn out on to a wire rack, strip off paper. Sandwich with the jam and sprinkle with caster sugar, or fill and top with fudge icing or buttercream.

# Strawberry Cake

A light sponge cake which is delicious for a special summer tea, or as a party dessert.

MAKES ONE 18–CM (7–IN) CAKE

60 g (2½ oz) plain flour
3 eggs

125 g (4 oz) caster sugar
40 g (1½ oz) melted butter

*For filling*
125 g (4 oz) strawberries
caster sugar

150 ml (¼ pint) double cream,
  whipped

Set oven to 190°C (375°F), gas mark 5. Grease and line two 18–cm (7–in) sandwich tins. Make whisked sponge mixture as described for swiss roll, page 59, folding in the melted butter after folding in the flour. Divide mixture between the two tins. Bake for 20–25 minutes, until sponge springs back when pressed lightly with the fingertips. Turn out on to wire rack, strip off lining paper and leave until cold. Wash and thinly slice strawberries, sprinkle with caster sugar. Spread one sponge with half the cream, put strawberries on top, then cover with remaining cream. Place second sponge on top and sprinkle with caster sugar.

# Swiss Roll

60 g (2½ oz) plain flour
3 eggs
125 g (4 oz) caster sugar

125 g (4 oz) warmed raspberry
jam
caster sugar to dredge

Set oven to 200°C (400°F), gas mark **6**. Grease and line a 33 × 23 cm (13 × 9 in) swiss roll tin. Sift flour. Half fill a large saucepan with water and bring to the boil. Break eggs into a large bowl and place over pan. Whisk eggs lightly; add sugar. Whisk for 10–15 minutes until very thick and fluffy and mixture will hold trail of whisk for 3 seconds. Remove bowl from saucepan. (It is not necessary to whisk eggs over hot water if using a table mixer, and this only takes 5 minutes.) Gently fold in a quarter of the flour; repeat with remaining flour. Pour into tin, bake for 8–10 minutes. Turn out on to a piece of greaseproof which has been sprinkled with flour. Leave to cool. When completely cold, trim crisp edges of swiss roll, spread with jam and roll up. Sprinkle with caster sugar.

# Sugarless Fruit Cake

In this cake a purée of dates is used instead of sugar: it's rich in vitamins, minerals and fibre and lower in calories than sugar. But the taste is excellent: no one ever guesses that there's any difference.

MAKES ONE 20-CM (8–IN) CAKE Ⓕ

225 g (8 oz) self-raising
    wholewheat flour
1 teaspoon mixed spice
175 g (6 oz) cooking dates,
    chopped
150 ml (5 fl oz) water
125 g (4 oz) soft margarine

grated rind of 1 lemon
3 eggs
450 g (1 lb) mixed dried fruit
25 g (1 oz) ground almonds
25 g (1 oz) flaked almonds

Set oven to 180°C (350°F), gas mark 4. Grease and line a 20–cm (8–in) deep cake tin. Sift flour with spice. Put dates into a pan with the water and heat until reduced to a purée. Cool. Put all ingredients except flaked almonds into a bowl and beat until thick and fluffy: 3–5 minutes. Turn into tin, sprinkle with almonds, bake for 2–2½ hours. Cool on wire rack.

# Traditional Victoria Sandwich Cake

Although creamed cakes can be made by the quick all-in-one method, nothing can beat the texture and keeping qualities of a Victoria sandwich cake made by the traditional method.

MAKES ONE 18–CM (7–IN) CAKE Ⓕ

175 g (6 oz) self-raising flour
175 g (6 oz) softened butter
175 g (6 oz) caster sugar
3 eggs, beaten

1–2 tablespoons water
3 tablespoons raspberry jam
icing or caster sugar to dredge

Set oven to 180°C (350°F), gas mark 4. Grease and line two 18–cm (7–in) sandwich tins. Sift flour. Cream butter and sugar until very light and fluffy, then gradually add the eggs, beating well after each addition. Fold in the flour. Divide mixture between the tins, smooth tops. Bake for 25–30 minutes: the cake should spring back when pressed lightly. Cool on wire rack, then sandwich with jam and dredge with caster or icing sugar.

# Index

Additional flavourings for cakes   10
All-in-one fruit cake   29
    method   14
    sponge   30
Almond and cherry ring   31
    paste   23
    paste, to coat cake with   19–21

Baking the cake   17
Banana cake with curd cheese and raspberry filling   32
Bramble cream cake   33
Buttercream, simple   23–4
Butterfly cakes   34

Cake(s), baking the   17
    freezing   18
    mixing the   13–16
    storing   18
    tins, buying   5–6
    tins, preparing   10–12

Carrot cake   35
Cherry ring, almond and   31
Chocolate cake   37
Christmas cake   38
Coconut and orange cake   39
Coffee and walnut cake   41
Creaming method   13–14
Curd cheese icing   24

Dried fruit, choosing and using   9–10
Dry ingredients   · 7
Dundee cake   42

Eggs, choosing and using   9
    sponge cake without   56
Equipment   5–6

Fat, types to use   7–8
Filling and icing cakes   18–24
Flavourings, additional   10
Flour, types to use   6–7

62

Freezing cakes   18
Frosted walnut layer cake   43
Frosting, seven-minute   26
Fruit cake, all-in-one   29
   nutty   50
   sugarless   60
Fudge icing   25

Gingerbread   44
Glacé icing   25

Icing, curd cheese   24
   fudge   25
   glacé   25
   royal   26
Icing the cake, filling and   18–24
Icings, recipes for   21–7
Ingredients, choosing   6–10
   preparing   13
Introduction   5

Lemon daisy cake   46
Liquid sweeteners, using   8
Liquids, for cake-making   9

Madeira cake   47
Making the cake   10–18
Marble cake   48

Melting method   16
Mixing the cake   13–16
Mocha cake   49

Nuts, for cakes   10
Nutty fruit cake   50

Orange cake, coconut and   39
Oven, preparing   13

Parkin   51
Preparing cake tins   10–12
Preparing ingredients   13
Preparing oven   13

Raising agents, types to use   7
Ring, almond and cherry   31
Rock cakes   52
Rose cake   53
Rough-ice, how to   21–2
Royal icing   26
Rubbing-in method   14

Seven-minute frosting   26
Simnel cake   55
Simple buttercream   23–4
Sponge, all-in-one   30
Sponge cake without eggs   56

Storing cakes 17
Strawberry cake 57
Sugar, types to use 8
Sugarless fruit cake 60
Swiss roll 59

Tins, how to put mixture in 16
Traditional Victoria sandwich
cake 61

Victoria sandwich cake,
traditional 61

Walnut cake, coffee and 41
layer cake, frosted 43
Whisking method 16

*Lincoln hm'*

*Ward 64*

*Bed 19*

*11 till 8 @ 12*